Real Stories From My Time

Felicity™ **THE BOSTON TEA PARTY**

By Rebecca Paley

With Felicity stories by Valerie Tripp

Illustrated by Kelley McMorris

Scholastic Inc.

Published by Scholastic Inc., *Publishers since 1920.* SCHOLASTIC and associated logos are trademarks and/or registered trademarks of Scholastic Inc. The publisher does not have any control over and does not assume any responsibility for author or third-party websites or their content.

Special thanks to Benjamin L. Carp

Photos ©: back cover: Library of Congress; 12, 13: North Wind Picture Archives; 15: Library of Congress; 23: North Wind Picture Archives; 31: Library of Congress; 34: Historia/REX/Shutterstock; 41, 44: Library of Congress; 45: Alfredo Dagli Orti/REX/Shutterstock; 47, 70: Library of Congress; 79: North Wind Picture Archives; 83, 90, 94: Library of Congress; 102: MPI/Getty Images.

Book design by Suzanne LaGasa

Library of Congress Cataloging-in-Publication Number: 2017049568

americangirl.com/service

ISBN 978-1-338-14893-0

10 9 8 7 6 5 4

19 20 21 22

Printed in the U.S.A.   23
First printing 2018

Real Stories From My Time

America's past is filled with stories of courage, adventure, tragedy, and hope. The Real Stories From My Time series pairs American Girl's beloved historical characters with true stories of pivotal events in American history. As you travel back in time to discover America's amazing past, these characters share their own incredible tales with you.

CONTENTS

Chapter 1

What Was the Boston Tea Party?

December 16, 1773. As day broke in Boston, thick clouds covered the city. A bone-chilling rain kept many of its sixteen thousand residents huddled under wool blankets in their houses. One by one they rose, stoking the coals in their fireplaces to stir up a bit of heat. Soon they'd put the kettles on for cups of . . . something warm.

What they really wanted was a cup of tea. Throughout the thirteen **colonies**, or the

1

original thirteen states, the belly-warming brew was a favorite drink. And not just on cold winter mornings—on hot summer afternoons, too, and crisp fall evenings, and rainy spring days. Anytime was teatime for the colonists of the New World. In fact, they consumed up to one million pounds a year.

At least, they did until all the trouble started brewing. In those days, the American colonies belonged to Britain, so they had to live by King George III's rules, which wasn't so bad at first. But then Britain started running out of money, so King George decided to impose all sorts of **taxes** on the colonists. The money the tax agents collected would go to Britain.

But instead of giving in to King George's demands, many colonists decided to fight back. Still, other colonists remained loyal

British subjects. These people were called "friends of government."

Many **Patriots**, who were people against British control of the colonies, lived in the city of Boston. Patriots there often led loud marches protesting King George's taxes. One tax in particular made the Patriots really angry: the tea tax. This was an extra fee the colonists had to pay for all tea shipped in from England.

Many Patriots decided to **boycott** English tea, which means that they refused to buy it. Others made threats against the tax agents whose job it was to collect the tax added on to the cost of the tea.

But tea from England kept coming, including a huge shipment that crossed the Atlantic Ocean in the fall of 1773. Three ships, packed with crates of tea, sat off the docks in Boston Harbor. Because of the fight over the tea tax, no one would unload the shipment.

All over the city, **handbills** were posted to trees and buildings that read, "Friends! Brethren! Countrymen! That worst of plagues, the detested TEA . . . is now arrived in this harbor." For three weeks, Patriot leaders asked the ships' captains to turn around and sail back to Britain. But the British captains wouldn't budge.

December 16, 1773, was the deadline. If the ships remained in the harbor, the colonists would have no choice but to pay the tea taxes—or be **fined** or thrown in jail. Yet the Patriots refused to back down. They believed the freedom of the colonies was at stake.

"If we give in to this unfair tax from King George, more injustices will surely follow," angry Patriots warned.

As the people of Boston emerged from

their houses that frigid December morning, and looked at the tea-laden ships looming in the harbor, little did they know that the events of the day, which would come to be known as the Boston Tea Party, would lead to the birth of the United States of America.

The story of Felicity Merriman starts in 1773, just before the American Revolution. Felicity is a spunky girl growing up in the city of Williamsburg, in the colony of Virginia. She loves helping her father in his general store. Lately, though, Felicity has heard heated arguments in her father's store. Some customers resent paying taxes to the king of England. Others believed that the colonists must obey their king no matter what. Also, many of the goods that flow into Mr. Merriman's store from all over the world—such as tea, tableware, and fine silk—cost more now because they come from England. The higher prices make the customers unhappy.

Hoping to speak to other importers and merchants and find a solution to this problem, Mr. Merriman and Felicity are sailing from Virginia up to the big city of Boston, Massachusetts.

Boston Harbor is a large port, and many of the goods shipped from England to the colonies arrive first in Boston. Because of this, Boston has become the site of protests against England and the king. Little do Felicity and her father know that they are sailing into the most dangerous adventure of their lives.

Although Felicity is a fictional character, her story will help you understand why the Boston Tea Party happened and imagine what it was like to be there.

November 27, 1773

Father and I are sailing to Boston on a ship called the *Dove*. Whenever I'm on deck, I lean into the wind and my cloak billows out behind me, just like the *Dove's* sails. The salty spray stings my face. I love it! Still, I'll be glad to get to Boston tomorrow and see Uncle George, Aunt Charlotte, and Cousin Charles. Cousin Charles is sixteen now and has a horse of his very own!

Father is eager to meet with Uncle George, his brother. Uncle George imports goods from England, and he supplies our store with many fine things to sell. But Father is worried. Those imported goods are more expensive every day, and Father is afraid he'll go into debt buying them for the store. Already, he has had to raise his prices, and his customers are unhappy. On top of the higher prices, now the customers have to pay a tax on tea, and we drink lots of tea. I do hope Uncle George can help Father find a way to get tea and other imported goods to sell in our store at lower prices so that our customers are happy again.

Chapter 2

New World, New Freedoms

Almost two hundred years before the Boston Tea Party, Europeans were exploring and claiming parts of what they called the New World. North America's east coast was rich in natural resources. Once forests were cleared, the land could be used for grazing and for growing corn (which the Native Americans were already growing!), beans, and other crops. So Europeans began to settle there in the 1500s.

Life in the New World wasn't easy for the

11

early European settlers. Many died from disease or starvation during the long and **treacherous** trip across the ocean. Those who survived the voyage often became sick with diseases such as malaria and yellow fever. When they tried to claim land that Native American Indians had been living on for thousands of years, they found that the Indians would not give up the land without a fight.

By the start of the 1600s, enough Europeans were living in the New World that they began to set up colonies. They were

A drawing of early European settlers fighting with Native American Indians

known as colonists. Colonists are people who leave their homelands to live in places that are often far away.

The first British colony was set up in Jamestown, Virginia, on May 14, 1607. Life in Jamestown was hard for the settlers, who struggled to grow food and find clean drinking water. Mosquitoes and other insects carried diseases. Out of the one hundred colonists who settled in Jamestown, eighty became ill and died within the first three years.

After the initial hardships, the Virginia

A drawing of the Jamestown colony in Virginia

colony began to grow and thrive. The settlers were able to plant tobacco plants, and they made money selling the plants' leaves to tobacco companies back in England.

Thirteen years later, in 1620, another group of English settlers landed on Plymouth Rock, about six hundred miles north of Jamestown. These settlers, known as Pilgrims, established Plymouth Colony.

The first Plymouth settlers arrived on a three-masted ship called the *Mayflower*. Many people thought girls weren't strong enough to make the hard trip across the ocean and then survive the harsh conditions of life in the New World. Despite that common belief, there were eleven girls aboard the *Mayflower* in 1620 as it sailed to Plymouth Rock. The youngest, Humility Cooper, was only a year old!

The oldest girl on the *Mayflower* was Priscilla Mullins, who made the trip with her father, mother, and brother when she was about seventeen years old. Priscilla was the only one in her family to survive the first cold and brutal Massachusetts winter.

In 1629, the Massachusetts Bay Colony was founded by about four hundred settlers. Its numbers quickly grew. By 1640, as many as twenty thousand settlers had arrived from England to join the new colony. Like many of the settlers before them, they had braved the long journey and the tough life of settling in a strange and wild land because in England they weren't allowed to worship God the way they wanted to. The official religion,

A drawing of the *Mayflower*

the Church of England, was against their particular form of Christianity.

Religious freedom was one reason people traveled to the New World. There were also those who wanted a say in their local government and to be allowed to vote. Any white male landowner could vote and have a say in the government, which wasn't the case back in England.

There was another good reason to come to the New World: It offered new ways to make money. The land was rich in natural resources like trees for fuel and lumber and animals for food and fur. Many settlers were farmers. Some built mills along rivers for sawing lumber and grinding wheat and corn. Others pulled cod, lobsters, whales, and other sea life from the mighty Atlantic Ocean.

Still, life was hard for the colonists. In Boston, there were outbreaks of smallpox, a painful disease that caused sores all over the body and was often **fatal**. Food could be hard to grow in the rocky soil. The Great Boston Fire of 1760 destroyed nearly 350 buildings and left more than a thousand people without homes. Still, despite the many hardships they faced, the British colonies in Boston and beyond continued to grow.

November 28, 1773

We sailed into Boston Harbor today. The *Dove* docked at Griffin's Wharf next to another ship that also arrived today, called the *Dartmouth*, which had sailed all the way from England. I saw a stern group of men lined up on the wharf like stone statues. When the crew tried to unload cargo from the *Dartmouth*, the men blocked their way. "We don't want your tea!" one shouted.

"What is this trouble?" Father asked Uncle George as he hurried us away from the wharf.

"We colonists have demanded that the *Dartmouth*—and its cargo of tea—return to England immediately. We don't want to sell the tea and pay the tax on it," Uncle George explained. "But the king's man, Governor

Thomas Hutchinson, has refused our demand."
Uncle George sighed. "We're in for a fight now."

It seems the fight is not only at the wharf. As
we walked through the streets, I saw two British
soldiers in red coats. Uncle George said the
king has sent soldiers to Boston to police the
colonists, which they don't like.

Aunt Charlotte welcomed us into her house
with a cup of tea. "Mind you, it's not real tea—it's
brewed from herbs I grew in my garden," she said.
"We drink no tea from England in this house."

I can see that the Boston Merrimans are
Patriots. A feeling begins to grow in my heart:
sympathy for the Patriot cause.

Chapter 3

Fighting the French and Indians

By 1755, there were nearly two million British living in the thirteen colonies. The colonies were: Delaware, Pennsylvania, New Jersey, Georgia, Connecticut, Massachusetts Bay, Maryland, South Carolina, New Hampshire, Virginia, New York, North Carolina, and Rhode Island and Providence Plantations.

These colonists weren't the only Europeans who had claimed land in the New World. There were also sixty thousand colonists from France living in North America. Although this was a much smaller population than the British colonists, the French controlled a lot of land.

French settlers were very interested in North American furs, because they knew that furs from beaver, bear, fox, and mink would sell for a lot of money in Europe. As a result, the French formed important friendships with the Ottawa, Shawnee, and other Indian tribes, who trapped the animals or traded with other tribes for the pelts. The French bought the furs from the Indians and sent them on ships back to Europe, where they were sold for a nice **profit**.

As the fur trade grew, the French started to claim more land in North America. But the British wanted that land, too. Small **skirmishes** broke out between the two nations. In 1754, war was declared.

At first, it looked as though the French

ndians trading with French settlers

would win the war. They had a bigger army in the New World, and many Native Americans fought on their side. For the first four years of the war, the French and Indians won battle after battle against the British. The members of the British government, however, didn't seem too concerned. Back in Britain, the feeling was "Let Americans fight Americans."

But one British statesman, William Pitt, saw the importance of winning the war that had become known as the French and Indian War. He eventually convinced **Parliament**, the name for the British government, to put him in charge of the war and to give him all the money he needed.

That was the turning point in the conflict. Pitt took advantage of the fact that Britain was much richer than France at the time. The British Royal Navy was also far superior to the French navy. And the British colonies themselves were a major source of food as well as fighters. Soon the tide of war had turned in Britain's favor. Some Shawnee Indians even decided to switch sides to fight with the British.

On September 8, 1760, the French soldiers, along with their remaining Indian allies, laid down their weapons and surrendered.

It took three years for Britain and France

to work out the terms of the surrender, but finally, on September 3, 1763, the Treaty of Paris was signed. France had to give up almost all the land it had claimed in North America.

It was a major victory for Britain. And many back home assumed it meant that the flag of Britain would fly over the British colonies in North America forever.

However, the war had left Britain with enormous **debts**. Parliament came up with a solution: It would tax the colonists to make up the debt. After all, Parliament reasoned, if not for the British military, the colonists would all be under French rule now.

Yet the colonists did not see it that way. They had fought hard and bravely to defend their lives and liberty. Many believed that they would do just fine without the support of the mother country. The fact that Britain now expected them to pay for that support was more than they could bear.

November 28, 1773

Just outside Uncle George's house is a handbill nailed to a tree trunk. It says angry things about the king of England and the tea tax, and announces a public meeting to discuss what to do about the shipload of tea in the harbor. It almost seems as if the people of Boston are itching to stir up trouble.

I can't help thinking of my grandfather, whom we visit every summer. Grandfather was born in England and came to the Virginia colony as a young man. He loves the king of England and is loyal to him. He says that although we live in America, England is our mother country, so we are all British subjects and should feel proud and glad to be so. Grandfather would not like the critical things that the people of Boston are saying about our mother country. Charles told me that some people have even started to secretly say that we should break free and declare our independence from Britain.

I know that Grandfather would call that **treason**. Oh, it is all so confusing! Grandfather loves and respects the king, and I love and respect Grandfather—but I am not sure I can agree with him. Still, I believe that we can be on different sides of the matter, and still love each other.

Stamp Act

Chapter 4

Taxation without Representation

The rulers in Britain didn't listen to the colonists. They wanted to collect more money from them—no matter what! On April 5, 1764, Parliament passed the Sugar Act. The act put a tax on sugar and molasses that were brought in from non-British foreign colonies. The act also lowered the tax on sugar and molasses that were brought in from British colonies. This meant that the colonists had to buy these goods from the British West Indies, or pay more money in tax. Or the colonists could smuggle in sugar and molasses.

But there was a problem: The Sugar Act cracked down on smuggling, making it harder to sneak in the goods. So the colonists were forced to buy from the British West Indies. The colonists, however, did not think that the British West Indies could produce enough molasses for their needs. Rum makers relied on molasses to make their product. So if it cost more to make the rum, the price for rum would have to go up. And if the price went up, then fewer people could afford to buy rum, thereby putting many rum makers out of business.

The Sugar Act also put a tax on indigo, a blue dye used to color cloth. In Boston, some merchants decided to stop ordering fine clothing and other luxury goods from Britain. Others went about their usual business. They figured the tax would be lifted.

Britain, however, was only getting started with its taxation of the colonies. On March 22, 1765, Parliament passed the Stamp Act, and it forced colonists to pay taxes on all printed papers, including newspapers, books, marriage licenses, legal contracts, and playing cards. Some members of Parliament thought this new tax went too far, but supporters pushed it through anyway.

As word reached the colonies of the new

Colonists protesting the Stamp Act

tax, a protest movement formed practically overnight. Throughout the colonies, angry crowds marched. At towns along the coast, ships carrying the dreaded stamps used to enforce the tax were prevented from docking.

The protests grew larger and louder as the summer went on. One of the most vocal groups was the Sons of Liberty. The members of the group included lawyers, merchants, and master craftsmen. Some of these men published articles in newspapers or pamphlets that described their points of view. These articles were often read out loud in taverns and other public places where other men were convinced by their arguments and joined the cause against the Stamp Act.

On August 14, 1765, the Sons of Liberty met to protest the taxes and hung an image of the city's stamp tax agent, Andrew Oliver, on a branch of a tree. The mob took torches to the **effigy**, or image, lighting it on fire. But that wasn't enough to satisfy their rage. They marched to Oliver's home and broke windows and tore down his fences. Then some men burst in the door, probably wanting to confront Oliver, but he wasn't there.

The Sons of Liberty targeted the highest elected officials, including Thomas Hutchinson, lieutenant governor of the Massachusetts Bay Colony and a firm friend of the government. On August 26, an angry mob showed up at his home and smashed down the front door with an ax. Others climbed through broken windows. They took everything they could get their hands on, including clothing, silver, and paintings. They might have taken Hutchinson himself had he not escaped in the nick of time to a neighbor's house. "Such ruins were never seen in America," Hutchinson later wrote of the attack on his house.

Thomas Hutchinson

Back in Britain, word of the violence and protests shocked many in Parliament. They viewed America as a "rebellious child" who needed to be punished.

In the end, Britain decided to **repeal** the Stamp Act on March 18, 1766. They took it back because the protests were hurting British companies financially. However, the war over taxation without **representation** was far from over.

November 28, 1773

My cousin Charles knows that I love horses, so after I unpacked, he took me to visit the stable, where he let me brush his horse, Mercury.

"Mercury is a fine horse," I said. "You have raised him well."

"We've raised each other," said Charles. "I've had Mercury since he was a colt and I was a lad. Look, I'll show you." Charles unlocked a cupboard, drew out a leather pouch, and handed me a document. "This is the bill of sale from when Father bought Mercury for me eight years ago, in 1765."

"What's this bumpy part?" I asked, rubbing my finger over a raised design stamped on one corner of the paper.

Charles frowned. "That," he said, "is British robbery."

What an odd thing to say! "What do you mean?" I asked him.

"The Stamp Act," Charles explained. "We colonists had to pay a tax on any official paper, like bills of sale, newspapers, contracts, even playing cards. This stamp is proof that the tax was paid."

"Playing cards? But that seems silly," I exclaimed. "Why would anyone pass such a petty law?"

"Greed," said Charles. "That's the reason for all the king's unfair taxes."

"Is it still the law?" I asked. Father sells playing cards in his store, and I don't remember seeing any stamps on them.

"No," said Charles. "Mother and Father and others protested so hard that the Stamp Act was repealed. But the injustice of it won't ever be forgotten." He sighed. "And the British just keep demanding other taxes, like the tax on—"

"*Tea*," we said together.

It's no wonder the Patriots' anger is boiling over, like a kettle that's been on the fire too long. And it's no wonder my sympathy for the Patriots' cause is growing stronger, too.

Chapter 5

A Massacre in Boston

The Green Dragon Tavern on Union Street in Boston's North End was always a lively place. On one night, the mood in the smoke-filled public house was especially rowdy. A group of young men, including blacksmiths, cabinetmakers, printers, and cobblers, were huddled in a corner, banging their mugs of ale and puffing on their pipes. The owner of the tavern let them be, knowing the men needed to blow off some steam. After all, this was the meeting of the Boston chapter of the Sons of Liberty, and the men had a lot to be angry about.

The shouts and protests grew louder as one of the men stood to speak. He was in his mid-forties and wore shabby clothes and a cheap wig. His hands trembled. Who was this man? This was Samuel Adams, one of the fiercest Patriots in the colonies. He was extremely well educated, having studied at Harvard College. Though he could have made a lot of money, perhaps working as a lawyer, Adams was not interested in wealth or things like a nice house and fancy clothing. All he cared about was justice and liberty for the colonists in America. Adams was tireless in his fight for freedom. When he wasn't leading protest marches or holding meetings at the local tavern, he was writing letters to newspapers like the *Boston-Gazette and Country Journal* to express his opinions on freedom and the British government. His writings also appeared in broadsides, large sheets of paper that were tacked to walls, posts, and trees. Adams's writings and speeches were so **persuasive** that he was known in Britain as "the most dangerous man in Massachusetts." The British disliked Adams for his ability to convince colonists that **independence** from English rule was best for their future. They feared—and respected—the way Adams's

Samuel Adams

fiery speeches inspired the colonists to take action.

Addressing his fellow Sons of Liberty at the Green Dragon Tavern, Adams whipped the men into a frenzy with his account of the British Parliament's latest attack on liberty: the Townshend Acts. Named for Charles Townshend, the British official who introduced the new measures to Parliament, the acts called for new taxes on British goods entering the colonies. This time, colonists would have to pay extra money on products like glass, paint, and tea.

The men left the tavern that night wanting more than ever to fight for their freedom. They no longer wanted to be under British control. Meanwhile, Britain sent more troops to the colonies to suppress the protests and ensure that its inspectors and agents could collect the new taxes.

Tensions between the two groups quickly grew. Throughout the colonies, Patriots continued to boycott British products. Many also continued their violent behavior.

In the spring of 1768, a mob rioted when John Hancock's ship was seized by a tax collector. Hancock, one of the Sons of Liberty and a well-known smuggler of wine, had docked his ship (called—what else?—*Liberty*) in Boston Harbor. The chief customs agent, Joseph Harrison, suspected Hancock had broken the law and wanted to inspect his ship. So he enlisted the help of two British warships that were in the harbor. While British sailors tied the *Liberty* to one of their ships, angry Boston residents gathered on the docks to protest. Later, a mob vandalized the home of one of the customs officers and even burned one of their boats!

Back in England, King George was

John Hancock

growing more and more frustrated with the actions of his "rebellious child." In 1768, he decided to send a message by dispatching four thousand troops to Boston, a city with fewer than seventeen thousand residents. The presence of so many Redcoats, as the troops were known because of their bright red uniforms, angered the people of Boston.

King George III, circa 1768

By 1770, fights between Patriots and **Loyalists** were becoming more common. Teenagers would taunt the British soldiers, calling them names and pelting them with rocks, oyster shells, rotten eggs, or whatever they could get their hands on. On the afternoon of March 5, 1770, one of these skirmishes broke out between a group of boys and some British soldiers.

One of the boys shouted an insult at the British soldiers. Another boy packed a snowball and hurled it at the officer. None of the boys were armed, but the soldiers were probably on edge because a few days earlier, a mob of angry Bostonians had beaten up a group of off-duty British soldiers.

As more Patriots joined the crowd, the scene became increasingly tense. Another round of snowballs was thrown at the soldiers. Despite repeated warnings from the troops, the crowd refused to break up.

Then, all of a sudden, someone shouted, "Fire!" A nervous soldier fired his gun, thinking that the order came from his captain. Other soldiers did the same, filling the air with gun smoke. When the smoke cleared, three colonists were dead and many more were injured.

Five Patriots died that day. The first person killed was Crispus Attucks, a runaway slave who had started a new life in Boston as a sailor. He is considered the first **casualty** of the American Revolution. More than twelve thousand people came to the funerals of Attucks and his fellow victims.

As tragic as the event was, Samuel Adams saw in it the opportunity to stir up more **resentment** toward the British. He began referring to the incident as the Boston

Crispus Attucks

Massacre. He later wrote, "The country shall be independent and we will be satisfied with nothing short of it."

One of Adams's friends was Paul Revere, who was well-known as a talented **silversmith**. He had learned the art from his father, who died when Paul was nineteen. Revere was also an excellent horseman—a talent that would come in handy during the later battles between the British and the colonists. But his first involvement with the Patriots came through his work as a copperplate engraver. In addition to the business cards and store signs that Revere engraved, he created political cartoons etched into and printed from sheets of copper.

After the Boston Massacre, Revere made a cartoon of the event, showing British troops opening fire on a group of innocent colonists. It wasn't a totally accurate depiction of the event, but it succeeded in making the Patriots even angrier toward the British.

King George, however, was not about to give in to all the anger and protests. If anything, he was prepared to hit back even harder.

Chapter 6

Teatime

Although coffee would eventually become America's favorite hot beverage, the people of the thirteen colonies were all about their tea. They loved sipping the hot water steeped in the carefully cured leaves, which were grown in China and shipped to America from England and other parts of Europe.

Some colonists believed that tea had the power to help the sick get better, while others simply liked the taste. But they all drank it daily, and often a few times a day. The wealthy served it in beautiful tea sets made of china. Afternoon tea was a social event where people gathered in their parlors or kitchens to gossip or discuss politics. Formal invitations might have been sent out to guests, but food was rarely on the menu. The custom of serving pastries like crumpets, cakes, and scones along with tea service didn't develop until the 1800s.

Despite the lack of snacks, the tea party was definitely a status symbol that allowed the lady of the house to display all the silver on her **elaborate** tea tray as she prepared the perfect brew. Even children hosted their own tea parties now and then.

Samuel Adams enjoyed a cup of tea in the morning and at night as much as the other Patriots. That's part of the reason they were so angry when the Tea Act—a law giving one British company control over all the tea traded in the colonies—was passed by

Parliament on May 10, 1773. The East India Company, a British company that sold tea from Asia all over the world, had fallen on hard times and wasn't making as much money as it used to. Why? One reason is because the company had an oversupply of tea. They had produced too much and were not selling enough. The colonies were drinking cheaper Dutch tea that was smuggled in. By the mid-1700s, nearly three-quarters of the tea consumed in America was smuggled. That took a major toll on the East India Company's profits.

The situation came to a boil in 1772 when the East India Company was stuck with eighteen million pounds of unsold tea. Something had to be done, or the tea would rot away in its warehouse and the company might go out of business.

Members of the British government wanted to help the East India Company because it was a very important part of England's **economy**. So Parliament passed the Tea Act. It said the colonists could only buy tea from the East India Company.

When the colonists learned of the Tea Act, in the fall of 1773, they were furious. Although this wasn't a tax, it was yet another instance of England telling the colonists what they could and couldn't do. And most colonists were sick and tired of Britain's costly rules. They wanted the freedom to make their own decisions.

In cities up and down the coast, including Boston, New York, and Philadelphia, protesters urged tea merchants to stop trading with the East India Company. When East India tea showed up in stores, the protesters boycotted them. A women's organization, the Daughters of Liberty, started making alternative "Liberty Tea" out of herbs and flowers such as rose hips. The Daughters of Liberty also participated in the protests and riots started by the Sons of Liberty. Additionally, when there was a shortage of fabric, the Daughters of Liberty organized "spinning bees," where groups of women transformed the lonely chore of spinning wool into a fun group activity. On one occasion, nearly one hundred Daughters of Liberty gathered with their wheels in a Newport, Rhode Island, meetinghouse, where they spent the day spinning 170 **skeins** of yarn that could be made into fabric.

Meanwhile, the Sons of Liberty continued to organize and plot. In Boston, a chapter of the organization, led by Samuel Adams, met daily to discuss what they should do about the situation. Yet no matter how angry the Patriots grew, King George and Parliament refused to repeal or take back the Tea Act.

In September 1773, seven British ships loaded with 2,000 wooden chests containing 600,000 pounds of tea set sail for the colonies.

News of the ships loaded with tea and headed their way enraged Boston's residents. A mob took to the streets and made for the home of Richard Clarke, one of the East India Company's local merchants. When they reached his house, they started breaking windows. Clarke and his family, hiding inside, were terrified. The protesters didn't stop their rioting until someone in the house fired a gun into the crowd.

Such intimidating tactics by protesters were successful in New York, Philadelphia, and Charleston. In those cities, all the agents for the East India Company quit by November. Protesters sent letters to East India Company agents in Boston ordering them to quit their jobs, too. "Fail not at your own peril," the letters warned. But Boston agents continued to work for the tea company. This was partly because Thomas Hutchinson, the governor of Massachusetts, lived in Boston and remained loyal to Britain, and so the agents—who included two of Hutchinson's sons—felt protected.

Weeks passed. The autumnal New England air grew colder, and the standoff between the Patriots and Loyalists of Boston grew more intense. Repeated messages were sent to Governor Hutchinson, demanding that he instruct the seven ships to turn around rather than docking in Boston. But Hutchinson refused to act.

More meetings were held, more protests carried out. But no agreements were reached. Finally, on November 28, 1773, one of the ships, the *Dartmouth*, arrived in Boston Harbor. It carried 144 chests of "that worst of plagues, the detested TEA, shipped for this Port by the East-Indian Company," announced a handbill that was posted all over Boston to stir up the colonists' anger.

For Patriots and Loyalists alike, the huge cargo vessel docked in Boston was too big to be ignored. The ship was a constant reminder of everything they were fighting over. The tension between British rule and Colonial liberty, heating up for years, was about to reaching a boiling point.

December 8, 1773

Now there are *two* ships in Boston Harbor laden with tea! I saw them, looming and gloomy, by the wharf this morning, when Aunt Charlotte and I went shopping to buy a special gift for Mother. "Oh, please may we go in this shop?" I asked Aunt Charlotte. "Look at the lovely china bowl in the window."

Aunt Charlotte hesitated but followed me inside.

"Charlotte Merriman!" said the shopkeeper. "I haven't seen *you* in many a long while. You're one of the Daughters of Liberty, who spin their own wool and make their own fabric and clothing rather than buying taxed goods from England, are you not?"

"I am," said Aunt Charlotte.

The shop owner smiled smugly. "And yet here you are in my shop," said she.

"My niece admires the bowl in your window," said Aunt Charlotte.

"That's a fine bowl, indeed," said the shopkeeper. "'Twas made in Wedgwood, England."

"Made in England?" said Aunt Charlotte. Her voice was steady but firm. "Shame on you for selling frippery and finery that's come from Britain, just like the tea on those hateful ships in our harbor. Don't you support the Patriots' fight for justice?"

My heart swelled with pride to hear my aunt stand on her beliefs, and I promised myself that I, too, would always stand strong for what I believed was right. But the shopkeeper was having none of it.

"Have you no loyalty to our king?" she asked. "Besides, everyone knows that if those ships are not sent back to England in the next eight days, British agents will seize the tea and start selling it—and charging the tax on it. No, I won't stand against the king, and nor should you if you've any common sense."

"I have something better than common sense," said Aunt Charlotte. "Principles. I believe the Patriots are right."

"Humph," snorted the shopkeeper. She turned to me and asked, "Do you want to buy this bowl?"

"No, thank you," I said politely. Suddenly, the bowl from England didn't look lovely to me anymore.

Chapter 7

The Night of the Party

On the morning of November 29, 1773, the people of Boston woke to the sound of church bells ringing throughout the city to signal an emergency. Many left their homes and filed into the streets to investigate.

A meeting was being held at the Old South Meeting House, on the corner of Milk and Cornhill Streets, to discuss the arrival of the *Dartmouth*. More than five thousand people descended on the brick meetinghouse,

Boston's largest building at the time. Huge crowds of people spilled onto the street.

The meeting lasted for two days. The stench from unwashed bodies was intense, and people had to stamp their feet and huddle close to keep warm. But with the fate of the colonies hanging in the balance, none of that seemed to matter.

Colonial leaders, including Samuel Adams, explained the situation. The law stated that the tea from the *Dartmouth* had to be unloaded and all the taxes paid within twenty days. The Patriots did not want that tea, and certainly did not want to pay the taxes! They were determined to find a way to beat the king at his own game.

The Sons of Liberty stationed guards at Griffin's Wharf to make sure no chests left the ship. More guards were posted when a second ship, *Eleanor*, arrived on December 2, and a third ship, *Beaver*, entered port on December 15.

Messages were sent to Governor Hutchinson, demanding that he send the ships back to Britain. He refused.

The mood throughout Boston darkened. Tensions flared, and nerves grew tense. Patriots and Loyalists who passed one another on the street could hardly look each other in the eye.

In the days leading up to the deadline, the Sons of Liberty held secret meetings. They reached a difficult decision: The tea had to be destroyed if they wanted to avoid paying taxes and giving in to British rule.

The morning of December 16 finally arrived. A cold drizzle fell as the people of Boston assembled one last time at the Old South Meeting House. The leaders voted to make a final appeal to Governor Hutchinson.

Francis Rotch, whose family owned the *Dartmouth*, was sent to Hutchinson's home outside the city. He would ask for permission to remove his ship from the harbor with the tea on board. Rotch was expected back by three o'clock that afternoon. But as the sun set over Boston, there was still no sign of him. The crowd grew restless.

Finally, around six o'clock, Rotch returned to the hall. His slumped body language told the bad news even before he opened his mouth. The governor would not give in. The tea would remain. And in just six hours, the colonists would be forced to pay up.

Samuel Adams took to the podium and declared, with a quiver in his voice, "This meeting can do no more to save the country!"

As if on cue, a round of whoops and whistles rang out from the balcony at the back of the meeting hall. As the people looked around, they saw that many of the men were disguised as Mohawk Indians, their faces painted with soot and grease and blankets draped over their shoulders. The costumes were a symbolic gesture meant to show the colonists' loyalty to America, as the Indians were native to the land.

"Boston Harbor is a teapot tonight!" someone shouted.

"Who knows how tea will mingle with salt water?" another asked.

As the crowd poured onto the street, the Sons of Liberty looked on with a combination of pride and fear. "Let every man do what is right in his own eyes," said John Hancock, one of the Sons of Liberty's most distinguished leaders. He said it knowing full well that the men before him were prepared to take action and defy the British.

At first, a few dozen protesters carrying axes, hatchets, and tomahawks marched down Milk Street. Others joined the mob along the way, and by the time they reached the harbor, they numbered nearly one hundred.

The most prominent Sons of Liberty, including Samuel Adams and John Hancock, were too recognizable, so they stayed behind. Instead, young carpenters, bricklayers, butchers, and smiths, like Joshua Wyeth, a sixteen-year-old blacksmith, carried out the mission. A young man named Samuel Sprague was on his way to a date with a girl when he was swept up in the crowd. He had no disguise handy, so he blackened his face with soot from a nearby stovepipe. Peter Slater was just fourteen years old and a rope maker's **apprentice**. He witnessed the scene from his upstairs bedroom, where his employer had locked him in. Rather than miss the excitement, he knotted his bedsheets into a long rope and used it to climb down the building. By the time the crowd reached the wharf it numbered anywhere from 60 to 120 men. Most of the people who took part in the raid were young. Only nine men were older than forty, and sixteen of them were still teenagers like Peter.

At about seven o'clock, the Patriots reached the ships. They were quiet so as not to attract attention from the British warships anchored in the harbor. On the dock, nearly one thousand onlookers had gathered, standing stone silent.

The Patriots split into three groups, one for each of the three ships. Once on board, the crew scurried belowdecks. Using pulleys and ropes, the Patriots hoisted the huge chests of tea, each weighing around 320 pounds, up from the cargo area and onto the deck. They split open the chests with axes, slashed through the tough canvas bags, and dumped the tea leaves overboard.

Since the tide was out, the water in the harbor was only a few feet deep. After a while, the tea began to pile up, so a handful of teenage boys were sent into the harbor to stir the leaves into the water.

The men hardly spoke as they worked. "No noise was heard except the occasional clink of the hatchet," wrote sixteen-year-old Samuel Cooper in one of only four known accounts by participants. "Before ten o'clock that night the entire cargo of the three vessels were deposited in the docks."

The men swept the decks clean so that not a single leaf remained. They even took off their shoes and shook any leaves from them.

The Boston Tea Party in progress

Not without regret, though. As Samuel Cooper wrote, "Many a wishful eye was directed to the piles of tea, which lay in the docks." One Patriot made the mistake of hiding a fistful of tea in the lining of his coat. The coat was ripped from his body and tossed into the muddy water.

No tea meant no tea.

As the Patriots made their way from the ships back onto the wharf, one of them pulled out a musical instrument called a fife and played a tune. The men were exhausted and **exuberant**.

December 16, 1773, late afternoon

This afternoon, Charles, Uncle George, Father, and I went to a meeting about the ships with their unwelcome cargoes of tea. When the crowd of nearly 5,000 people heard that the governor still refused to send the ships back to England, they grew angry. I heard one man shout, "Boston Harbor is a teapot tonight!"

Afterward, as we walked home behind Father and Uncle George, Charles whispered to me, "I'm going to help toss that tea off those ships tonight."

"I am, too," I told him. He started to protest, but I said, "I may be just a child, but I'm going, and that's that!"

December 17, 1773, after midnight!

Just after dusk last night, Cousin Charles and I met in the stable. I dressed in breeches to be disguised as a boy and for freer movement. Charles and I darkened our faces with soot from the fireplace so that we'd be hard to see and recognize. It was full dark when we joined the group headed to Griffin's Wharf.

"March quietly," came the murmured order.

I froze with fear when I saw why: British Royal Navy warships were patrolling the harbor.

Nearly one thousand silent souls stood at the shoreline. "They're here for our protection," said Charles. "The British soldiers won't trouble an innocent crowd."

At the dock we split into three groups, one for each boat. As Charles and I boarded the *Dartmouth*, a strong voice said to the captain, "Go belowdecks, sir. We will do you no harm." My knees shook, and Charles nudged me. 'Twas Uncle George who spoke to the captain!

We set to work as quietly as shadows. I heard only the creaks of ropes and pulleys hoisting the chests of tea out of the ship's hold and then dull thuds as the chests were lowered onto the deck. Men broke open the chests with axes, slashed the canvas bags inside, and tossed the tea overboard in a blizzard of leaves. Men in canoes below beat down the floating tea so that it sank. It was my job to sweep tea off the ship's deck. I swept until my arms ached and my hands were blistered. We had been told, "Not one tea leaf is to be left anywhere. Every bit of tea is to be destroyed."

By ten o'clock, all was over. I handed my broom to one of the Dartmouth's crew, found Charles, and walked down the gangplank from the ship back onto the wharf. We joined the others marching back to town. We trudged home and went to the stable. I was glad to be in the serene presence of Mercury as we brushed the tea leaves off our coats and scrubbed the soot from our faces. I've never been so exhausted—or so elated. I have truly joined the fight for justice!

Chapter 8

The Party's Over

As day broke over Boston, tea leaves still blanketed the harbor and their aroma hung in the air. Though no Patriots spoke directly of the act, the mood in Boston was joyous.

Loyalists, of course, were not so happy, least of all Governor Hutchinson. He called the events of December 16 the "boldest stroke that had been struck in America."

News of the "destruction of the tea" spread quickly to the colonists, thanks to the horseback-riding heroics of Paul Revere. He was sent by the Sons of Liberty to tell as many colonists as possible about what had happened in Boston. Never one to shy away from a challenge, Revere took off from Boston the day after the Tea Party and rode to New York, where he arrived on December 21. All along the two-hundred-mile journey, he stopped at inns and taverns to tell the locals there about the destruction of tea. From New York, he rode another one hundred miles or so to the city of Philadelphia.

By the end of December, the event in Boston, later called the Boston Tea Party, was the hottest topic of discussion through-out the thirteen colonies.

It took several weeks for the news to reach Britain, since the news couldn't travel any faster than it took a ship to cross the ocean. Finally, on January 19, 1774, King George III got the full report from his advisers. And he probably wasn't very happy!

The king and Parliament decided to punish the entire city of Boston with the passage of the Coercive Acts, which the Patriots later called the Intolerable Acts. As one member of Parliament put it, "The town of Boston must be knocked down about their ears and destroyed." The British Parliament also passed these acts in the hopes that they would prevent other colonies from resisting or protesting their rule.

Paul Revere on horseback circa December 21, 1773

The Coercive Acts shut down Boston Harbor until the East India Tea Company was repaid for the destroyed tea. That meant that only food and firewood were allowed into the port. Everything else was banned—not even hay was allowed in to feed the starving horses. The people of Boston were forced to provide housing for the thousands of British troops sent there to enforce the new laws. So, many British soldiers slept in barns, taverns, and other buildings, making these places unusable for the colonists. And there was nowhere for them to complain since town meetings of any kind were outlawed.

At first, these acts did seem to make life in Boston so hard that the Patriots would be knocked down and destroyed as Parliament hoped. But then something incredible happened, something King George never could have expected. People throughout the colonies **rallied** to save Boston. The people of Windham,

Connecticut, sent 258 sheep to feed their starving neighbors in Boston. More food and supplies arrived from all over the colonies.

Official statements of support followed. "If our sister colony of Massachusetts Bay is enslaved we cannot long remain free," wrote representatives from Virginia. "United we stand, divided we fall."

Thomas Jefferson of Virginia added, "An attack on one of our sister colonies . . . is an attack on [us] all."

The leaders of the colonies knew they had to come together to determine their next steps. Each colony would send representatives, known as delegates, to a convention to decide their next move. The meeting was known as the First Continental Congress. It took place place on September 5, 1774, at Carpenters' Hall in Philadelphia. Fifty-six delegates from twelve colonies (Georgia was the only holdout) attended the meetings, which went on for several weeks.

By the middle of October, the congress decided to boycott almost all British goods until the Intolerable Acts were repealed. They drafted a statement, known as the Declaration of Colonial Rights, and sent it by ship across the Atlantic to King George III. It called for many freedoms from British rule.

The congress also agreed to meet again, on May 10, 1775. The delegates wanted to allow enough time for their demands to reach King George and for the British government to respond. Some of the delegates still believed that some kind of understanding could be reached between the colonies and Britain.

Others, like John Hancock, were not as optimistic. As early as November, just a month after the First Continental Congress, he was calling for twelve thousand men to volunteer as minutemen. The name came from the idea that they could be ready to fight in one minute. Patriots signed up—and started to stockpile gunpowder. Many Patriots agreed with John Hancock that the colonies should prepare for war—especially after King George sent back orders to crush any revolt.

War was clearly in the air—even if neither side had declared it. The mood was best summed up by Patrick Henry, a leader from Virginia, who announced in March 1775, "The war is actually begun! I know not what course others may take, but as for me, give me liberty! Or give me death."

The rallying call would soon echo throughout the land.

Patrick Henry

December 18, 1773

The *Dove* welcomed us back aboard and swept us away from Boston with billowing sails and wild, wintry winds. Father and I are sailing home, and I'm glad, for he says that if the winds cooperate, we'll be home in Williamsburg for Christmas. As we sailed out of Boston Harbor, I imagined that I saw tea leaves floating in the water. Perhaps I did, for Charles told me that enough tea was tossed to make many millions of cups of tea.

"Father," I said, "is there any hope for peace between the Patriots and the people still loyal to the king? I worry for Uncle George and Aunt Charlotte's safety if war comes. I'm especially afraid that Charles will go off to be a soldier and risk his life."

"'Tis right for a person to stand up

for what they believe in," said Father. He tilted his head and looked at me. "Even if she's just a young girl, who goes to a very unusual tea party and comes to breakfast the next morning with a tea leaf tangled in her hair."

I gasped. Charles and I were certain we had not been recognized! "F-Father—" I stammered.

"Hush," said Father. "You and I are both pledged to secrecy, and Uncle George and Charles are, too." He put his arm around my shoulder. "There's trouble ahead for our colonies," he said sadly. "It may be many years before our families are together again. It will be impossible for the Virginia Merrimans to see the Boston Merrimans for a long time, if war comes." He sighed. "And it will, I fear."

I fear that when the king finds out about the destruction of the tea, he'll be as fast and furious in his punishments—and just as impossible to stop—as the winds driving the *Dove* out to sea.

Chapter 9

The Shot Heard Round the World

Patrick Henry was right: The war had begun. British troops flooded the city of Boston. Under strict orders from General Thomas Gage, the soldiers were determined to find the leaders of the rebellion, including Samuel Adams and John Hancock. The soldiers also searched the colonists' homes for weapons and smuggled goods.

By the middle of April 1775, most of the leaders of the Sons of Liberty had managed to escape Boston. That made General Gage nervous. What if they were planning some sort of uprising? He couldn't have that happen.

Gage sent a **battalion** of soldiers to Lexington, a town about twelve miles northwest of Boston, where Adams and Hancock were rumored to be hiding. More soldiers were sent to Concord, a nearby town where the Patriots had stockpiled muskets, bullets, gunpowder, and other weapons. It was time to show the Patriots who was in charge.

The Sons of Liberty heard about Gage's plans on April 18, and thought it was another job for Paul. They were referring to Paul Revere, of course, the fearless horseman who could always be counted on to spread messages quickly. Along with a handful of other messengers, Revere jumped on his horse and rode through the night, warning colonial minutemen, from Boston to Concord, about the planned British attack.

Though the warning helped the colonists prepare, it didn't change the fact that the British vastly outnumbered them. The following morning, April 19, 1775, about seventy-five colonial fighters confronted several hundred British Redcoats in an open area called Lexington Green.

At first, the confrontation seemed harmless enough. A British officer ordered the group to break up and leave the green. There was some grumbling from the crowd. But tensions settled, and it looked as though the morning would pass without a shot having been fired.

All of a sudden, a gunshot pierced the air, followed by more gunfire. Eight Patriots lay dead, nine more were wounded, and a British solider was also injured. No one knows who fired the first bullet, but it came to be known many years later as "the shot heard round the world," since it was the first real battle of the American Revolution.

And there was more action to come that morning, as the British soldiers marched on to Concord. Though the Redcoats had had the advantage in Lexington, by the time they reached Concord, many more Patriots had arrived.

Now it was seven hundred British soldiers defending themselves against thousands of colonists. As they retreated to Boston, the

Artist's depiction of "the shot heard round the world"

Patriots continued to shoot at them from behind trees, walls, and houses. Although the British had the best-trained army in the world at the time, they were easy targets for men hidden from sight. Finally, the British soldiers ditched everything, even their weapons, to make a fast retreat. All total, 73 British soldiers were killed that day and another 174 were wounded. By comparison, 49 colonists died and 39 were wounded.

The Battles of Lexington and Concord ended in victory for the Americans. But they were just the beginning.

On July 4, 1776, the Continental Congress adopted the Declaration of Independence, in which the colonies formally declared their independence from England. For the next eight and a half years, British and American forces would be locked in a bloody war. As the war continued, there would be setbacks for the Patriots. At no point during the American Revolution was victory assured, and nearly seven thousand Patriots would make the ultimate sacrifice, losing their lives in battle. Even more died as prisoners of the British or from disease.

Although the British army and navy were larger and better trained, the colonists were more committed to their cause, plus they had help from the French and Spanish. In the end, the colonists' desire for freedom and self-rule proved stronger than the king's desire to keep control of his colonies. In 1781, az big part of the British army surrendered in Yorktown. But the British still occupied places such as Savannah, Georgia; Charleston, South Carolina; and New York, New York. When the Treaty of Paris of 1783 was signed, the thirteen colonies were no more. Instead, they formed a new country, which would be called the United States of America.

In time, the United States of America would grow to fifty states, and its democratic spirit would be a model for many other nations around the world.

A copy of the Declaration of Independence

July 28, 1776,
in Williamsburg, Virginia

The war Father and I feared came faster and
more furiously than any of us had imagined. We've
been at war for a year now, and the shelves in
Father's store look very different: Since ships
carrying goods from England are no longer coming
to the colonies, we've learned to get by with less.
But we colonists have also learned how to make
many of the things we used to import. I am proud
to see fabrics woven here in America in Father's
store. I like drinking rose hip tea and knitting with
wool I've spun myself—just as the Daughters of
Liberty do in Boston.

Today I heard the declaration written by the
First Continental Congress read aloud on

the steps of the courthouse boldly declaring our independence from British rule. No longer will we be subjects of the king, paying taxes we never agreed to, punished for disobeying laws imposed on us unfairly, and ruled by powers an ocean away. I felt shivers when I heard the words:

"We hold these truths to be self-evident, that all men are created equal, that they are endowed by their Creator with certain unalienable Rights, that among these are Life, Liberty and the pursuit of Happiness."

Father says the war for independence will be long and hard and full of loss and sorrow. I have no doubt that's true. But I also have no doubt that the struggle will be worth it in the end. For wasn't I there at the beginning, at that "very unusual tea party" up in Boston, with the first Patriots who stood up for freedom?

Glossary

Apprentice – a person who is learning a trade or skill

Battalion – a large group of soldiers

Boycott – to refuse to buy or use something as a way of protest

Casualty – someone injured, killed, or captured during war

Colonies – areas that are controlled by, or belong to, another country

Debts – things owed by one person or country to another

Economy – the way a country makes and uses goods and services

Effigy – a portrait, statue, or other image of a person

Elaborate – done with great care and a lot of detail

Exuberant – very, very happy

Fatal – causing death

Fined – made to pay a sum of money as a punishment

Handbills – small, printed advertisements

Independence – freedom from being controlled by another country or government

Loyalists – people faithful to the government, in this case Britain

Parliament – a group of people who are responsible for making laws

Patriots – people who love their country, in this case America

Persuasive – having the ability to get someone to believe or do something

Profit – the amount of money made by a business after all expenses are paid

Rallied – got ready for action

Repeal – to do away with or cancel

Representation – a person or group supporting another person or group

Resentment – bitterness or discontentment

Silversmith – a craftsman who makes or repairs objects made from silver

Skeins – coils of yarn

Skirmishes – short fights during war

Taxes – the amount of money that governments require people to pay, which is then used by the governments

Treacherous – dangerous

Treason – the betrayal of one's country

Source Notes

Freedman, Russell. *The Boston Tea Party*. New York: Holiday House, 2012.

Gondosch, Linda. *How Did Tea and Taxes Spark a Revolution?: And Other Questions about the Boston Tea Party*. Minneapolis: Lerner, 2010.

Krull, Kathleen. *What Was the Boston Tea Party?* New York: Penguin Group, 2013.

Marten, James, ed. *Children in Colonial America*. New York: New York University Press, 2007.

Tripp, Valerie, *Love and Loyalty: A Felicity Classic*, Volume 1. Wisconsin: American Girl Publishing, 2017.

Tripp, Valerie, *A Stand for Independence: A Felicity Classic*, Volume 2. Wisconsin: American Girl Publishing, 2017.

Trueit, Trudi Strain. *The Boston Tea Party: Cornerstones of Freedom*. New York: Scholastic, 2005.

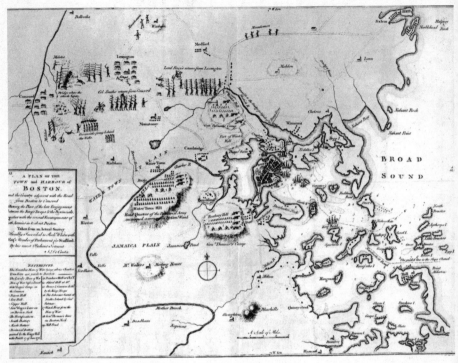
Boston during the start of the American War of Independence

Timeline

1600s – Britain sets up colonies along the northeast coast of North America

1760 – George III becomes King of Britain

1754–1763 – The French and Indian War is fought between France and Britain. The name refers to the fact that France received strong support from its Native American allies. Britain won the war, but not without going into big debt

1765 – The British government passes the Stamp Act, which requires colonists to pay taxes on certain paper documents

1767 – Britain passes the Revenue Act, nicknamed the Townshend Acts, which calls for a tax on tea, glass, paint, and more in the colonies

1768 – Around four thousand British troops are sent to Boston to control the growing resistance to the many new taxes

1770 – On March 5, five colonists are killed by British troops in Boston, in what would come to be known as the Boston Massacre

1773

> May 10 – Britain passes the Tea Act, calling for a tax of three cents per pound on all tea sent to the colonies

> November 28 – the first of three ships carrying tea from the British East India Company arrives in Boston Harbor

> December 16 – following weeks of protests and meetings, the Boston Tea Party takes place from 7:00 p.m. to 9:00 p.m.

1774

> March 30 – As a reaction to the Boston Tea Party, the British Parliament passes the Coercive Acts

> September 5 – Delegates from twelve of the thirteen colonies meet at the First Continental

Congress in Philadelphia to talk about how to respond to Britain's continued attack on political and personal freedoms

1775 – On April 19, the opening shots of the Revolutionary War are fired at the battles of Lexington and Concord

1776 – On July 4, colonists adopt the Declaration of Independence, officially declaring themselves free from British rule

1783 – The Revolutionary War ends, with America's final independence from Britain